CARNAL KNOWLEDGE

CARNAL KNOWLEDGE

The Sex Trivia Quiz Book

DON VAYLE

AVON BOOKS ◆ NEW YORK

CARNAL KNOWLEDGE is an original publication of Avon Books. This work has never before appeared in book form.

AVON BOOKS
A division of
The Hearst Corporation
1350 Avenue of the Americas
New York, New York 10019

Copyright © 1996 by Don Vayle
Cover art by Sebastian Kruger
Book design by Kellan Peck
Published by arrangement with the author
Library of Congress Catalog Card Number: 95-48026
ISBN: 0-380-78362-2

Library of Congress Cataloging in Publication Data:

Vayle, Don.
  Carnal knowledge : the sex trivia quiz book / Don Vayle.
      p.   cm.
1. Sex—Miscellanea. 2. Sex customs—Miscellanea. I. Title.
HQ25.v38 1996   95-48026
306.7—dc20   CIP

First Avon Books Trade Printing: July 1996

AVON TRADEMARK REG. U.S. PAT. OFF. AND IN OTHER COUNTRIES, MARCA REGISTRADA, HECHO EN U.S.A.

Printed in the U.S.A.

OPM 10 9 8 7 6 5 4 3 2 1

CARNAL
KNOWLEDGE

A college student loved showing off his sex organ, which he called *Jumbo*. He became United States President:

A. Bill Clinton

B. John F. Kennedy

C. Lyndon Johnson

◉◉◉◉◉◉◉

C. *Lyndon Baines Johnson was known to call his sex organ Jumbo. As a senator he was notorious for his sexual affairs.*

Who tried to grab a bunch of quick feels from Judy Garland on *The Wizard of Oz* set?

A. some of the Munchkins
B. the lion, Bert Lahr
C. the scarecrow, Ray Bolger

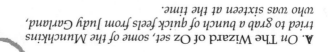

A. *On* The Wizard of Oz *set, some of the Munchkins tried to grab a bunch of quick feels from Judy Garland, who was sixteen at the time.*

Of the men who visit plastic surgeons for penile augmentation, how many have average-sized sex organs?

    A. 10%
    B. 25%
    C. 50%

6. Half the men who visit plastic surgeons for penile augmentation have average-sized sex organs.

Speaking of her sexual technique, Marilyn Monroe told Marlon Brando:

A. "I'm one of the best in Hollywood."
B. "I don't know if I do it right."
C. "You can't teach an old dog new tricks."

⑥⑥⑥⑥⑥⑥⑥

B. *Marilyn told Marlon, "I don't know if I do it right." Movie writer Nunnally Johnson said, "Copulation was, I'm sure, Marilyn's uncomplicated way of saying thank you."*

Women who go to rodeos seeking sex from cowboys are called:

   A. happy campers
   B. buckle bunnies
   C. cowgirls

B. Women who go to rodeos seeking sex from cowboys are called buckle bunnies.

Adolf Hitler had:

- **A.** just one testicle
- **B.** countless homosexual lovers
- **C.** a secret Jewish wife

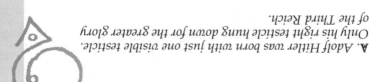

A. *Adolf Hitler was born with just one visible testicle. Only his right testicle hung down for the greater glory of the Third Reich.*

$\mathbf{B}$efore getting married, "Entertainment Tonight"'s John Tesh and Connie Selleca had a one-year courtship without sex because:

A. they are born-again Christians

B. Connie needed to clear up a sexual disease

C. John was impotent

🌀 🌀 🌀 🌀 🌀 🌀 🌀

A. *Before getting married, John Tesh and Connie Selleca did not have sex because they are born-again Christians.*

Before he became President of the United States, John F. Kennedy was a major stud in Palm Beach with the nickname:

A. Jack Rabbit
B. Mattress Jack
C. Jumper Jack

۞ ۞ ۞ ۞ ۞ ۞ ۞

B. *John F. Kennedy's nickname was Mattress Jack.*

Which man is *not* known for having a gigantic sex organ?

   A. the dictator Joseph Stalin
   B. the actor Milton Berle
   C. the mad monk Grigory Rasputin

@@@@@@@

A. Joseph Stalin did not have a gigantic sex organ. The mad monk Grigory Rasputin had this claim to fame as does comedian Milton Berle, who is known for having the largest sex organ in Hollywood.

After promiscuous teenager Amy Fisher shot Joey Buttafuoco's wife, she hired a lawyer who:

    A. was a former vibrating bed salesman

    B. tried to rape her

    C. was an ex-congressman

⑥⑨⑥⑨⑥⑨⑥

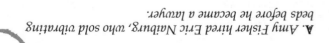

A. Amy Fisher hired Eric Naiburg, who sold vibrating beds before he became a lawyer.

Who helps the pornographic movie actor maintain his sexual readiness while the camera is not on?

A. the cookie girl
B. the sweet girl
C. the fluff girl

C. The fluff girl helps the male porn star stay ready for sex. For gay movies, fluff boys are used.

Will Rogers drilled a hole so he could peek into the dressing room of:

A. Shirley Temple
B. Ava Gardner
C. Betty Grable

☙ ☙ ☙ ☙ ☙ ☙ ☙

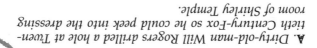

A. *Dirty-old-man Will Rogers drilled a hole at Twentieth Century-Fox so he could peek into the dressing room of Shirley Temple.*

Which woman had her breast serve as the mold for a drinking goblet?

A. Elizabeth Taylor
B. Marilyn Monroe
C. Marie Antoinette

C. Just before the French Revolution, Marie Antoinette had her breast serve as the mold for a drinking goblet.

According to *Playgirl* magazine, how many wives have had sex at least once when they didn't want it?

  A. 48%
  B. 72%
  C. 96%

@@@@@@@@

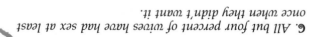

C. All but four percent of wives have had sex at least once when they didn't want it.

A United States congressman would most likely go to a call girl:

A. to humiliate her
B. to be humiliated by her
C. to ask for her vote

B. A congressman would most likely go to a call girl to be humiliated by her. Men of great power and control often pay for the kinds of sex that abuse and abuse them.

Associated with witchcraft, a succubus is:

- **A.** a female demon who has sex with men
- **B.** a demon who forces women into prostitution
- **C.** a demon who shows his genitals during church services

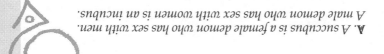

A. A succubus is a female demon who has sex with men. A male demon who has sex with women is an incubus.

In Palm Beach, the William Kennedy Smith defense against rape claimed that:

A. the woman was an ex-prostitute

B. taking off her panty hose meant that the woman "wanted it"

C. Uncle Ted made him do it

B. *The William Kennedy Smith defense against rape claimed that taking off her panty hose meant that she "wanted it."*

Amy Fisher claimed that Joey Buttafuoco could have sexual intercourse:

A. only in the missionary position
B. six to eight times a night
C. only in the dark

©©©©©©©

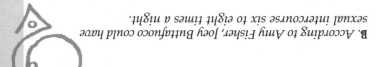

B. *According to Amy Fisher, Joey Buttafuoco could have sexual intercourse six to eight times a night.*

Who did Walt Disney say he loved more than any woman he ever knew?

A. Cinderella

B. Mickey Mouse

C. Howard Hughes

B. Walt Disney said he loved his own creation Mickey Mouse more than any woman he ever knew. The cartoon mouse began his career with the name Steamboat Willy.

After Lorena Bobbitt cut off her husband's sex organ, she:

- **A**. gave it to her pit bull
- **B**. threw it out the car window
- **C**. tacked it to a bulletin board

𝕲𝕲𝕲𝕲𝕲𝕲𝕲

B. *After cutting off her husband's sex organ, Lorena Bobbitt threw it out the car window. It was found by a volunteer fireman, who put it in a Ziploc bag.*

What do men hate most about being single?

    A. loneliness
    B. lack of sex
    C. lousy food

@@@@@@@@

A. *What men hate most about being single is loneliness. They are no different from women in this regard.*

After writing many erotic novels, like *Lady Chatterley's Lover*, D. H. Lawrence:

    A. preferred sex in books to sex in bed

    B. made his mother-in-law his mistress

    C. committed suicide out of guilt

಄಄಄಄಄಄಄

A. At age twenty-three, David Herbert Lawrence had his first sexual affair with the local pharmacist's wife. After writing many erotic novels, he preferred sex in books to sex in bed.

A man in *high drag* is dressed:

A. to look like a woman

B. to look like a man, but with women's things underneath

C. in leather and chains

☙☙☙☙☙☙☙

A. A man in high drag is dressed to look like a woman.

Who told British Prime Minister Harold Macmillan that if he didn't have non-marital sex at least once a day, he got a headache?

A. Winston Churchill

B. Prince Philip

C. John F. Kennedy

@@@@@@@

C. *President Kennedy told Prime Minister Macmillan that if he didn't have nonmarital sex at least once a day, he got a headache.*

Before Thomas Jefferson became President, he carried on a secret sexual relationship with Sally Hemings, who was:

A. bisexual
B. a slave
C. his niece

☺☺☺☺☺☺☺

B. *Thomas Jefferson carried on a secret sexual relationship with his teenage slave Sally Hemings.*

Sex goddess Marilyn Monroe made a habit of:

A. saying a prayer before sexual intercourse

B. wearing brand new panties every day

C. wearing no underclothes, on the movie set and off

⊚ ⊚ ⊚ ⊚ ⊚ ⊚ ⊚

C. *Sex queen Marilyn Monroe made a habit of not wearing underclothes—on the movie set and off. And she storied in advertising that fact.*

Who wrote, "I go into ecstasies every time I see the naked figure of a woman," in her diary?

A. Charlotte Brontë
B. Anne Frank
C. Anaïs Nin

☺☺☺☺☺☺☺

B. In her diary, Anne Frank wrote, "I go into ecstasies every time I see the naked figure of a woman."

Napoleon preferred making love to Josephine:

A. only when his mistresses were not handy

B. while she wore a military tunic

C. when she was unwashed

ⓖⓖⓖⓖⓖⓖⓖ

C. *Napoleon preferred making love to Josephine when she was unwashed. He was sexually obsessed with rear ends, and he said that Josephine had the prettiest one imaginable.*

H.G. Wells, who wrote *The Time Machine*, was sexually aroused for maybe the first time in his boyhood:

    A. by his family's Greek housemaid
    B. by his family's Greek gardener
    C. by Greek statues

@@@@@@@

C. *Young Herbert George Wells was sexually aroused by Greek statues. At age fifty he had a sexual affair with birth control advocate Margaret Sanger.*

Aphrodite, the Greek goddess of love and sexual intercourse

A. was born of her father's castrated sex organ

B. governed sex but never partook of it personally

C. had sexual intercourse with every major god

🌀🌀🌀🌀🌀🌀🌀

A. *Aphrodite was born of her father's castrated sex organ, which had fallen into the sea. She arose from the foam and was swept up on the shore of the isle of Cyprus.*

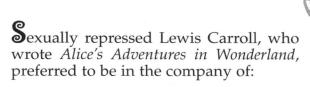

Sexually repressed Lewis Carroll, who wrote *Alice's Adventures in Wonderland*, preferred to be in the company of:

A. prostitutes
B. lesbians
C. ten-year-old girls

C. Lewis Carroll preferred the company of prepubescent girls. In their midst, his lifelong stammer would leave him.

To be a member of the Mile High Club you must make love:

- **A.** in an airplane
- **B.** under the influence of LSD
- **C.** during a mountain climb

@@@@@@@

A. To be a member of the Mile High Club you must make love in an airplane at an altitude of one mile or higher.

In 1993, romantic novels were what percent of all paperback sales?

A. 17%

B. 27%

C. 47%

⊚ ⊚ ⊚ ⊚ ⊚ ⊚ ⊚

C. *According to* Romantic Times *magazine, romantic novels were forty-seven percent of all paperback sales in 1993.*

In the movie *Barbarella*, Jane Fonda:

A. makes love while floating in a low-gravity field

B. wears a futuristic see-through bra

C. sexually tortures the English ambassador

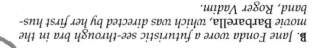

B. *Jane Fonda wore a futuristic see-through bra in the movie* **Barbarella,** *which was directed by her first husband, Roger Vadim.*

Being caught in the middle of a sexual act is called:

    A. *in flagrante delicto*
    B. *cogito, ergo sum*
    C. *sexualus arrestus*

©©©©©©©

A. *Being caught in the middle of a sexual act is called in flagrante delicto.*

How much was Marilyn Monroe paid for her nude calendar photo?

- **A**. $50
- **B**. $500
- **C**. $50,000

⑥⑨⑥⑨⑥⑨⑥

A. *Marilyn Monroe was paid fifty dollars for her nude calendar photo.*

Most American brothels that supply virgins:

A. import young virgins from foreign countries

B. have girls repeatedly fake their virginity

C. play Madonna's song "Like a Virgin"

@@@@@@@

B. *Most brothels supplying virgins have girls repeatedly fake their virginity, a trick that has been taught for thousands of years.*

Men who pimp for juvenile prostitutes are called:

A. girly men
B. popcorn pimps
C. big brothers

🌀 🌀 🌀 🌀

B. *Men who pimp for juvenile prostitutes are called popcorn pimps.*

Up to 50,000 homosexuals were sent to Nazi concentration camps, where each man:

A. was castrated

B. had his genitals electrically shocked

C. had to wear a pink triangle

⑥⑨⑥⑨⑥⑨⑥⑨

C. Homosexuals sent to Nazi concentration camps were made to wear a pink triangle.

If the Barbie doll were human, the bust measurement would be:

- **A.** 31 inches
- **B.** 35 inches
- **C.** 39 inches

@@@@@@@

C. If the Barbie doll were human, the bust measurement would be thirty-nine inches. Barbie was based on a sexy German doll that was based on a sexy-looking cartoon prostitute named Lili.

Little Richard, who's in the Rock and Roll Hall of Fame for songs like "Tutti Frutti," performed a second wedding ceremony for:

A. Michael Jackson and Lisa Marie Presley

B. Demi Moore and Bruce Willis

C. Elizabeth Taylor and Larry Fortensky

☺☺☺☺☺☺☺

B. *Little Richard performed a second wedding ceremony for Demi Moore and Bruce Willis.*

A *fag hag* is:

A. an older gay man with a much younger sexual partner

B. a heterosexual woman who likes to hang out with gay men

C. a bisexual woman

☙☙☙☙☙☙☙

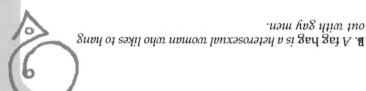

B. *A* **fag hag** *is a heterosexual woman who likes to hang out with gay men.*

Which country singer was sued by three women who claimed that he pressured them into playing kinky phone-sex games?

A. Randy Travis
B. Kenny Rogers
C. Garth Brooks

@@@@@@@

B. *Country singer Kenny Rogers was sued by three women who claimed he pressured them into playing kinky phone-sex games.*

Horatio Alger, a writer of rags-to-riches stories for boys, was fired from his position as minister of the Unitarian Church of Brewster, Massachusetts, because:

A. of his "over-fondness" for young boys

B. his wife's nymphomania became a public embarrassment

C. he couldn't resist exposing his bare bottom to little girls

⟲⟲⟲⟲⟲⟲⟲

A. Horatio Alger was fired from the Unitarian Church because his hands tended to roam when he ministered to little boys.

In the 1950s, teenage boys tuned their TVs to a kiddie show called "The Mickey Mouse Club" to see a young actress outgrow her Mouseketeer T-shirt. She was:

A. Sandra Dee

B. Annette Funicello

C. Mamie van Doren

⊚⊚⊚⊚⊚⊚⊚

B. *In the 1950s, teenage boys lusted after Annette Funicello.*

Who is more likely to walk in on someone having sex?

A. a hotel maid
B. a motel maid
C. Geraldo Rivera

☺☺☺☺☺☺☺

B. *A motel maid is more likely than a hotel maid to interrupt an "occupied" couple, because she usually has less training.*

Senator Gary Hart, while a presidential candidate, committed adultery aboard a yacht named:

A. *American Virtue*
B. *Monkey Business*
C. *Love Boat*

ⓖⓖⓖⓖⓖⓖⓖ

B. *While aboard Monkey Business, Senator Gary Hart allowed himself to be photographed with Donna Rice on his lap. The photo was sold to the National Enquirer.*

A high school boy is more likely to have a sexual fantasy about:

A. a movie star
B. a cheerleader
C. any girl he sits next to

C. An adolescent boy is more likely to fantasize about any girl he sits next to than about a movie star or cheerleader.

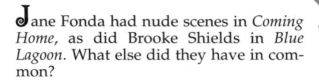

Jane Fonda had nude scenes in *Coming Home*, as did Brooke Shields in *Blue Lagoon*. What else did they have in common?

- **A.** both fully bared their breasts
- **B.** both used body doubles
- **C.** both had off-camera affairs with their leading men

B. *Both Jane Fonda and Brooke Shields used body doubles for their nude scenes.*

The first nude celebrity in *Playboy* magazine was:

A. Marilyn Monroe
B. Betty Grable
C. Jane Fonda

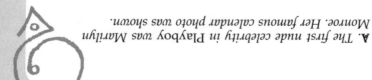

A. *The first nude celebrity in Playboy was Marilyn Monroe. Her famous calendar photo was shown.*

In the Cherokee language, female genitalia are called *tupuli*, which means:

A. hungry coyote
B. butterfly from God
C. feathered flying serpent

C. Tupuli, in the Cherokee language, means feathered flying serpent, one of their descriptions for female genitalia.

Which name means *young but sexually alluring*?

- **A.** Sensulla
- **B.** Lolita
- **C.** Babette

⊚⊚⊚⊚⊚⊚⊚

B. The name Lolita was created by writer Vladimir Nabokov to mean *young but sexually alluring*. When Amy Fisher got caught with Joey Buttafuoco, the press called her the "Long Island Lolita."

Sweet Julie Andrews, star of *Mary Poppins* and *The Sound of Music*, in a later film:

A. raised her dress above her head

B. completely bared her breasts

C. simulated sexual intercourse in a hot tub

B. *Julie Andrews completely bared her breasts in the movie* S.O.B., *directed by her husband, Blake Edwards.*

The first widely publicized sex-change operation took place in 1952, when an American ex-soldier became:

A. Christine Jorgensen
B. Betty Friedan
C. Virginia Woolf

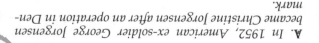

A. In 1952, American ex-soldier George Jorgensen became Christine Jorgensen after an operation in Denmark.

Who was the top pinup sex queen of the 1970s?

- **A.** Jane Fonda
- **B.** Dolly Parton
- **C.** Farrah Fawcett

C. With her long hair featured on millions of posters, Farrah Fawcett became the top pinup queen of the 1970s. Two decades later she posed totally nude for Playboy magazine.

Who did car dealers say they would most like to take for a ride?

A. Pamela Anderson

B. Heather Locklear

C. Drew Barrymore

@@@@@@@

B. *Car dealers at a convention said that the sexy star they'd most like to take for a ride is Heather Locklear, who calls herself a "world-class vixen on 'Melrose Place.'"*

For movie star Jane Russell, billionaire Howard Hughes claimed he designed:

A. a topless bathing suit
B. an aerodynamic bra
C. edible panties

⊚⊚⊚⊚⊚⊚⊚

B. *Howard Hughes claimed that he designed an aerodynamic bra to show off Jane Russell's cleavage in The Outlaw. He said, "There are two good reasons men will go to see her."*

In the smash hit *Ghost*, star Demi Moore

A. slipped Patrick Swayze her tongue in the kissing scenes

B. made Patrick Swayze wear a jock strap so his constant arousal wouldn't distract her

C. was filmed in full frontal nudity that was later cut from the film

@@@@@@@

A. In Ghost, *Demi Moore slipped Patrick Swayze her tongue in the kissing scenes, and she also said she slipped it to Rob Lowe in* About Last Night.

According to a *Seventeen* magazine poll, how many boys want to marry a virgin?

A. 3 out of 10
B. 5 out of 10
C. 8 out of 10

A. According to Seventeen, three out of ten boys want to marry a virgin.

Sex kitten Ann-Margret:

A. loved to ride topless on her motor-cycle in the desert

B. wore no panties under her cheer-leader's outfit in high school

C. displayed her ample bosom in the movie *Carnal Knowledge*

@@@@@@@

C. *Ann-Margret nakedly displayed her ample bosom to Jack Nicholson and the movie audience.*

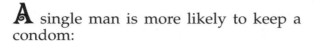

A single man is more likely to keep a condom:

    A. in his medicine cabinet
    B. in his billfold
    C. until it is brittle and cracked

◎◎◎◎◎◎◎

B. *A single man is more likely to keep a condom in his billfold than in his medicine cabinet even though a condom in a billfold may deteriorate past the point of safety in about one month.*

With whom did President John F. Kennedy *not* go to bed?

A. Mafia playgirl Judith Exner
B. actress Angie Dickinson
C. singer Nancy Sinatra

⊚⊚⊚⊚⊚⊚⊚

C. John F. Kennedy did not go to bed with singer Nancy Sinatra, but he did sleep with Judith Exner and Angie Dickinson.

Actress Clara Bow, famous for her lascivious wink, compared Gary Cooper's lovemaking equipment to:

A. a wet noodle

B. a horse

C. an ice cube

⊚⊚⊚⊚⊚⊚⊚

B. Clara Bow compared Gary Cooper's genitals to a horse. In fact, many top female stars in Hollywood insisted that young Gary be in their movies because of his endowment.

How many fixes of heroin can a New York City street prostitute buy with the wages of one sexual encounter?

A. one
B. three
C. five

A. From the wages of one sexual encounter, a New York City prostitute can buy one fix of heroin.

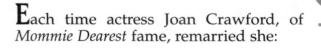

Each time actress Joan Crawford, of *Mommie Dearest* fame, remarried she:

   A. changed locks on the bedroom doors
   B. put in new toilet seats all over her house
   C. bought a new set of wire coat hangers

☺☺☺☺☺☺☺

B. *Each time Joan Crawford remarried, she put in new toilet seats all over her house.*

Nancy Reagan's godmother, the actress
Alla Nazimova:

 A. had an affair with Ronald Reagan's
    father
 B. was a lesbian
 C. directed pornographic movies

◎◎◎◎◎◎◎

B. *First Lady Nancy Reagan's godmother was a lesbian.*

W̲hich one of John F. Kennedy's sexual conquests did brother Ted make a play for?

A. Mafia playgirl Judith Exner

B. sexpot Marilyn Monroe

C. actress Angie Dickinson

@@@@@@@

A. Judith Exner said that about the same time she met President Kennedy, Teddy made a sexual play for her, but she turned him down.

$\mathbf{A}$ccording to *Ladies' Home Journal*, what's the number one thing a wife should do if her husband cheats?

    A. divorce him
    B. insist on counseling for both
    C. hire penis-slasher Lorena Bobbitt

©©©©©©©

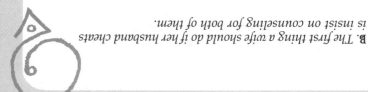

B. *The first thing a wife should do if her husband cheats is insist on counseling for both of them.*

A man who pays a prostitute just for talk, not for sex, is more likely:

A. to lecture her
B. to seek information
C. to sell her a Bible

A. A man who pays a prostitute just for talk is likely to deliver a stern moral lecture, which is sex enough for him.

Who is more likely to listen, through a motel wall, to a couple making love?

A. a young man alone

B. a young woman alone

C. a young man alone and a young woman alone are about equally likely

@ @ @ @ @ @ @

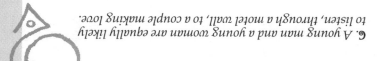

C. A young man and a young woman are equally likely to listen, through a motel wall, to a couple making love.

Although sex goddess Marilyn Monroe said that she liked to feel blond all over and dyed *all* her hair, her real color was

A. red
B. brown
C. black

@@@@@@@

B. *Although Marilyn Monroe was blond all over, her real hair color was brown.*

Which singing movie star was a wife swapper?

A. Dean Martin
B. Elvis Presley
C. Nelson Eddy

⑨⑨⑨⑨⑨⑨⑨

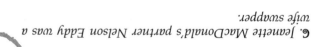

C. *Jeanette MacDonald's partner Nelson Eddy was a wife swapper.*

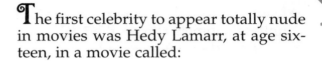

The first celebrity to appear totally nude in movies was Hedy Lamarr, at age sixteen, in a movie called:

- **A.** *Ecstasy*
- **B.** *And God Created Woman*
- **C.** *Tobacco Road*

@@@@@@@

A. *At age sixteen, Hedy Lamarr was the first celebrity to appear nude in the movie Ecstasy.*

Movie star Rudolph Valentino, who had countless women throw themselves at him, married two women who:

A. had been married to congressmen
B. refused sex after his death
C. were lesbians

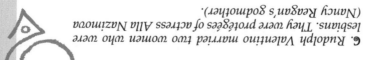

C. *Rudolph Valentino married two women who were lesbians. They were protégées of actress Alla Nazimova (Nancy Reagan's godmother).*

Which retailing chain sold the most *Playboy* magazines per month until a Christian boycott made them quit?

A. Kmart
B. 7-Eleven
C. Wal-Mart

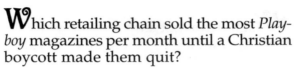

B. *7-Eleven sold the most Playboy magazines per month until a Christian boycott put a stop to it.*

Which actor got into trouble with the law for videotaping his sexual activities?

A. Rob Lowe

B. Pee-wee Herman

C. Jack Nicholson

⑥⑨⑥⑨⑥⑨⑥

A. Actor Rob Lowe got into trouble for videotaping his encounters with two women he picked up at the Democratic National Convention in Atlanta.

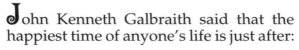

John Kenneth Galbraith said that the happiest time of anyone's life is just after:

A. the first kiss

B. the first sexual experience

C. the first divorce

@@@@@@@

C. John Kenneth Galbraith said that the happiest time of anyone's life is just after the first divorce.

Which black-haired movie and TV star began her career in pornographic magazines as a true redhead?

A. Joan Collins
B. Linda Gray
C. Elvira

⑥⑥⑥⑥⑥⑥⑥

C. *The dark-haired Elvira, Mistress of the Dark, began her career as a redhead. Those old pornographic photos are still being reprinted in skin magazines.*

When Elizabeth Taylor married construction worker Larry Fortensky, she was given away by:

A. Richard Burton, Jr.

B. Ronald Reagan

C. Michael Jackson

⑤⑥⑥⑤⑥⑥⑥

C. *Elizabeth Taylor was given away by Michael Jackson at his California property Neverland.*

Carly Simon's song "You're So Vain" is about:

A. Mick Jagger
B. Warren Beatty
C. James Taylor

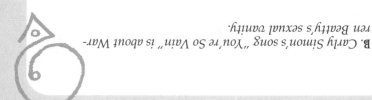

B. *Carly Simon's song "You're So Vain" is about Warren Beatty's sexual vanity.*

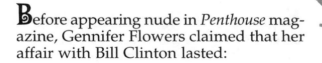

Before appearing nude in *Penthouse* magazine, Gennifer Flowers claimed that her affair with Bill Clinton lasted:

A. four months
B. four years
C. fourteen years

☺☺☺☺☺☺☺

C. *Gennifer Flowers claimed that her affair with Bill Clinton lasted fourteen years.*

English art critic John Ruskin refused to consummate his marriage after he made the horrible discovery that his new wife:

A. was already pregnant

B. was his half-sister

C. had pubic hair

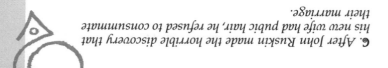

C. *After John Ruskin made the horrible discovery that his new wife had pubic hair, he refused to consummate their marriage.*

Which sex star dumped actor Kiefer Sutherland three days before the marriage?

A. Madonna
B. Drew Barrymore
C. Julia Roberts

@@@@@@@

C. *Julia Roberts of Pretty Woman fame dumped actor Kiefer Sutherland three days before the wedding.*

During sex, the father of comic actor Richard Pryor:

A. died

B. set his house on fire

C. broke his front teeth

☙ ❧ ☙ ❧ ☙ ❧

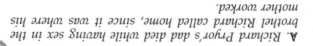

A. Richard Pryor's dad died while having sex in the brothel Richard called home, since it was where his mother worked.

Who is more likely to break up after becoming jealous?

- A. the man is more likely
- B. the woman is more likely
- C. the man and woman are about equally likely

A. *A man is more likely than a woman to break up after becoming jealous.*

Which composer had syphilis?

A. Ludwig van Beethoven
B. Wolfgang Mozart
C. John Lennon

☺☺☺☺☺☺☺

A. Ludwig van Beethoven had syphilis, which probably contributed to his deafness.

Sexpot Marilyn Monroe dropped out of high school at age fifteen:

    A. because she was pregnant

    B. because she was caught in the act with her history teacher

    C. to get married so she wouldn't have to stay in an orphanage or foster home

☙ ☙ ☙ ☙ ☙ ☙ ☙

C. Marilyn Monroe got married at fifteen so she wouldn't have to stay in an orphanage or foster home.

The first thing famous stripper Gypsy Rose Lee asked of every costume she wore was:

    A. "Are the shoes sexy?"
    B. "Do I show enough?"
    C. "Do I cover up enough?"

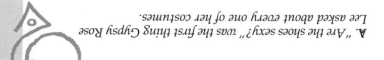

A. *"Are the shoes sexy?" was the first thing Gypsy Rose Lee asked about every one of her costumes.*

Mary Baker Eddy, founder of Christian Science, at age fifty-six:

A. lost her virginity

B. listed her age on the marriage certificate as forty

C. was arrested for seducing a fourteen-year-old boy

🌀 🌀 🌀 🌀 🌀 🌀 🌀

B. Mary Baker Eddy lost her virginity at fifteen. She married at twenty-four. At age fifty-six, she listed her age on the marriage certificate as forty. In her eighties she suggested celibacy as the true spiritual condition.

Alexander Dumas, author of *The Three Musketeers*, died:

- **A.** in a duel over his mistress
- **B.** when a jealous husband pushed him off a roof
- **C.** of syphilis

⊚⊚⊚⊚⊚⊚⊚

C. *Alexander Dumas died of syphilis. He once said, "I need several mistresses. If I had only one, she'd be dead within a week."*

What did the Mayflower Madam say men wanted her high-priced call girls to wear?

A. crotchless panties

B. seamed stockings

C. hats

C. The Mayflower Madam said that men wanted her girls to wear hats, presumably as a matter of dignity and class.

What did ex-Avenger, actress Diana Rigg, do to shorten her love scenes with George Lazenby when he played James Bond?

- **A.** she ate garlic
- **B.** she invited George's wife to the movie set
- **C.** she stepped on his toes

A. Diana Rigg ate garlic to shorten her love scenes with George Lazenby.

The hot new item of 1966 was:

A. the bikini
B. edible panties
C. the miniskirt

🌀🌀🌀🌀🌀🌀🌀

C. *The hot new item of 1966 was the miniskirt, which immediately was seen in movie after movie.*

After Tom Cruise divorced her, actress Mimi Rogers:

 A. moved in with her lesbian lover
 B. married Tom's best friend
 C. posed nude for *Playboy* magazine

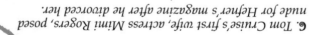

C. *Tom Cruise's first wife, actress Mimi Rogers, posed nude for Hefner's magazine after he divorced her.*

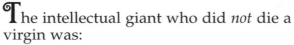

The intellectual giant who did *not* die a virgin was:

- **A.** mathematical genius Sir Isaac Newton
- **B.** philosopher genius Immanuel Kant
- **C.** physicist genius Albert Einstein

ⓒⓖⓒⓖⓒⓖⓒ

C. Sir Isaac Newton and Immanuel Kant were both virgins when they died, whereas Albert Einstein had gained carnal knowledge.

The first feature film that was an X-rated cartoon was

   A. *George the Dog*
   B. *Tweety the Bird*
   C. *Fritz the Cat*

⊚ ⊚ ⊚ ⊚ ⊚ ⊚ ⊚

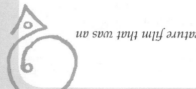

C. Fritz the Cat *was the first feature film that was an X-rated cartoon.*

Who was the Queen of Sheba's lover?

A. King David
B. King Solomon
C. Stephen King

⊚ ⊚ ⊚ ⊚ ⊚ ⊚ ⊚

B. *King Solomon had hundreds of wives and hundreds of concubines, but his most famous lover was the Queen of Sheba.*

Marlene Dietrich, the first actress to portray a lesbian kiss in the movies, had an affair with which war hero?

A. General Dwight Eisenhower
B. General Douglas MacArthur
C. General George Patton

◉◉◉◉◉◉◉

C. Sultry bisexual actress Marlene Dietrich had an affair with General George Patton.

The leader of Adolf Hitler's Storm Troopers, Ernst Röhm:

A. always made love with his socks on

B. was a homosexual

C. chose the Nazi swastika for its sexual symbolism

@@@@@@@

B. *Homosexual Ernst Röhm led Adolf Hitler's Storm Troopers until Hitler had him killed for being gay.*

Joan Crawford, the sexually omnivorous actress, got teed off when her sexual advances were turned down by:

A. Elvis Presley

B. John F. Kennedy

C. Marilyn Monroe

⊚⊚⊚⊚⊚⊚⊚

C. *Joan Crawford got angry when her sexual advances were turned down by Marilyn Monroe. Later, Joan sniped, "I don't think Marilyn has a friend. She hasn't taken time to make a friend in this industry."*

Who said that his role in *A Killing Affair* was the first time White America accepted a black man in bed with a white woman on the screen?

- **A.** Sidney Poitier
- **B.** Denzel Washington
- **C.** O.J. Simpson

⊚⊚⊚⊚⊚⊚⊚

C. *Actor O.J. Simpson said that he was the first black man in bed with a white woman in a movie that America accepted.*

What's the main reason women don't ask men for dates?

- **A.** they're afraid men will think it's a sexual come-on
- **B.** they're afraid of rejection
- **C.** they think it's immoral

೯೦೯೦೯೦೯

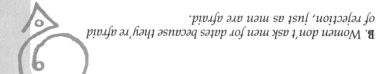

B. *Women don't ask men for dates because they're afraid of rejection, just as men are afraid.*

Which manic-depressive actor liked getting beaten and kicked as a sexual thrill?

A. Liberace
B. Rock Hudson
C. James Dean

☺☺☺☺☺☺☺

C. *James Dean liked getting beaten and kicked as a sexual thrill. He occasionally had men stub out their cigarettes on his chest.*

When are women more likely to feel the urge to commit adultery?

- **A.** when their ovulation cycle makes them fertile
- **B.** when their ovulation cycle makes them infertile
- **C.** when the Democrats are in the White House

@@@@@@@

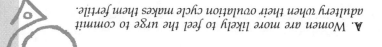

A. *Women are more likely to feel the urge to commit adultery when their ovulation cycle makes them fertile.*

The most famous female evangelist, Aimee Semple McPherson, had a discreet sexual affair with which entertainer?

A. Milton Berle
B. Clark Gable
C. Lucky Luciano

@@@@@@@

A. Aimee Semple McPherson, who baptized Marilyn Monroe, had an affair with Milton Berle in front of a homemade altar with crucifix and candles.

Which sex star did *not* appear in an X-rated movie?

A. Mae West
B. Raquel Welch
C. Jayne Mansfield

🌀🌀🌀🌀🌀🌀🌀

C. Jayne Mansfield did not appear in an X-rated movie, but Mae West and Raquel Welch both appeared in the X-rated Myra Breckinridge, in which Raquel rapes a man with a dildo.

When painter Peter Paul Rubens was fifty-three, he married a woman who became his nude model. She was:

A. sixteen years old

B. schizophrenic

C. sixty-one years old

☺☺☺☺☺☺☺

A. *Peter Paul Rubens married a sixteen-year-old girl who became his nude model.*

Actress Debra Winger said that the sexiest thing in the world is to be totally naked:

A. with a younger man
B. with your wedding band on
C. with a stranger

☺☺☺☺☺☺☺

B. Actress Debra Winger said that the sexiest thing in the world is to be totally naked with your wedding band on.

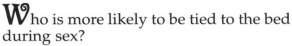

Who is more likely to be tied to the bed during sex?

   A. the husband
   B. the wife
   C. Pee-wee Herman and Judge Wapner

⊚⊚⊚⊚⊚⊚⊚

A. The husband is more likely than the wife to be tied to the bed during sex.

Sonja Henie, Norwegian Olympic ice skating champion and Hollywood movie star:

- **A.** had a sexual affair with heavyweight boxing champion Joe Louis
- **B.** got sexually aroused whenever she smelled pancakes cooking
- **C.** remained a virgin until she married

@@@@@@@

A. Sonja Henie had a sexual affair with heavyweight boxing champion Joe Louis. Just like Mae West, Sonja had a strong sexual preference for black prizefighters.

The cactus that is used by some cultures to enhance erotic play is:

A. saguaro
B. aloe
C. peyote

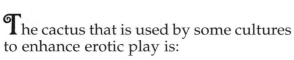

C. *In Central and South America, peyote is used to enhance erotic play.*

In the giant old-growth forests of north-western United States, ten-inch Banana Slugs:

A. for their size, have the largest sex organs of any land animal

B. for their size, have the smallest sex organs of any land animal

C. end their thirty hours of hermaph-roditic mating by chewing off each other's male sex organs

@@@@@@@

C. *The ten-inch Banana Slugs of the Northwest end their thirty hours of hermaphroditic mating by chewing off each other's male sex organs.*

Norwegian playwright Henrik Ibsen, who wrote *A Doll's House*:

A. liked to have sex outdoors in freezing weather

B. loved to sing while having sex

C. felt guilty because he couldn't perform sexually

C. Henrik Ibsen felt guilty because he couldn't perform sexually. A recurring theme in his plays is sexual repression.

In which country does an unmarried thirty-year-old woman have the smallest chance of marrying?

A. Denmark
B. Germany
C. the United States

ⓖⓖⓖⓖⓖⓖⓖ

Russian writer Fyodor Dostoyevsky:

A. got sexually aroused whenever he ate eggs

B. was attracted to feet in a sexually obsessive way

C. said that homosexuality was a gift from God

〰️〰️〰️〰️〰️〰️〰️

B. *Dostoyevsky was attracted to feet in a sexually obsessive way. According to Psychology Today, so are about one and a half million active foot fetishists in America.*

When a Washington, D.C., politician goes to a call girl, how often does he choose plain sexual intercourse?

A. about 10% of the time
B. about 30% of the time
C. about 50% of the time

☺☺☺☺☺☺☺

A. *When a politician goes to a call girl, he chooses plain sexual intercourse only about ten percent of the time.*

Who was known as the husband of every woman and the wife of every man?

A. Rock Hudson

B. Alexander Ramsbottom

C. Julius Caesar

◉◉◉◉◉◉

C. The month of July was named for Julius Caesar, who was known as the husband of every woman and the wife of every man.

To whom was Katharine Hepburn referring when she said, "It's a new low for actresses when you have to wonder what's between her ears instead of her legs?"

A. Madonna
B. Sharon Stone
C. Jayne Mansfield

☺☺☺☺☺☺☺

B. Katharine Hepburn was referring to Sharon Stone when she said, "It's a new low for actresses when you have to wonder what's between her ears instead of her legs."

Raspberry Tart, Bachelor's Wife, and Painted Cat are:

- **A.** synonyms for prostitute
- **B.** sex toys
- **C.** Oriental sexual positions

⊚⊚⊚⊚⊚⊚⊚

A. *Raspberry Tart, Bachelor's Wife, and Painted Cat are synonyms for prostitute, and the word prostitute means "to expose for sale."*

Who has the easiest time picking up women?

A. handsome men
B. rich men
C. poor men

☺☺☺☺☺☺☺

B. Although rich men have the easiest time picking up women, they have no advantage when it comes to sexual satisfaction.

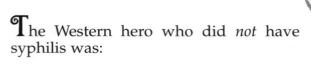

The Western hero who did *not* have syphilis was:

    A. General George Custer
    B. Wild Bill Hickok
    C. Wyatt Earp

🌀🌀🌀🌀🌀🌀🌀

B. *Western hero Wyatt Earp did not have syphilis, but General George Custer and Wild Bill Hickok both had the disease.*

Isaac Singer, inventor of the sewing machine:

A. was sexually aroused by the kiss of the whip
B. fathered eight legitimate and seventeen illegitimate children
C. asked his wife for a divorce while retaining bed privileges

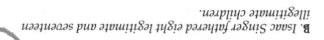

B. *Isaac Singer fathered eight legitimate and seventeen illegitimate children.*

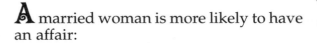

A married woman is more likely to have an affair:

    A. if she lives in a big city
    B. if she lives in a village
    C. if she lives next door to Judge Ito

ⓖ ⓖ ⓖ ⓖ ⓖ ⓖ ⓖ

A. A married woman is more likely to have an affair if she lives in a big city than if she lives in a village.

For love poems and erotic poetry, inspiration comes from a muse named:

A. Elizabeth Barrett Browning
B. Erato
C. Sappho

B. *For erotic inspiration, poets look to the muse Erato, one of nine Greek goddesses who preside over the arts.*

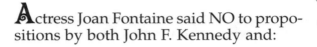

Actress Joan Fontaine said NO to propositions by both John F. Kennedy and:

A. his brother Bobby
B. his brother Teddy
C. his father Joe

☺ ☺ ☺ ☺ ☺ ☺ ☺

C. *Joan Fontaine said NO to sexual advances made by John F. Kennedy and his father, Joe.*

To save energy for the camera, who has no sex while filming a movie?

A. Meryl Streep
B. Elizabeth Taylor
C. Jack Nicholson

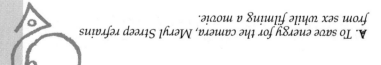

A. To save energy for the camera, Meryl Streep refrains from sex while filming a movie.

A nude or seminude picture of a man is called:

    A. beefcake
    B. pound cake
    C. layer cake

             ☺ ☺ ☺ ☺ ☺ ☺ ☺

A. A nude or seminude picture of a man is called beef-cake, while a nude or seminude picture of a woman is called cheesecake.

Roger Staubach, Hall of Fame quarterback for the Dallas Cowboys, said that he enjoyed sex just as much as "Broadway Joe" Namath, but he enjoyed it:

    A. with just one woman
    B. in private, as God intended
    C. with his wide receivers

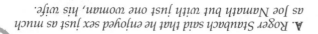

A. Roger Staubach said that he enjoyed sex just as much as Joe Namath but just with one woman, his wife.

Many famous early jazz musicians, like Louis Armstrong and Jelly Roll Morton, got their starts:

   A. working as pimps
   B. selling pornography
   C. playing music in brothels

🌀🌀🌀🌀🌀🌀🌀

C. *Many early jazz musicians got their starts playing music in brothels.*

Actress Shelley Winters says that her old roommate, Marilyn Monroe, during her early days in Hollywood, fantasized about having a child with

A. Winston Churchill
B. Albert Einstein
C. Harry S. Truman

☺☺☺☺☺☺☺

B. According to Shelley Winters, Marilyn Monroe fantasized about having a child with Albert Einstein. His brains and her looks, Marilyn hoped.

W riter James Joyce, whose books were often banned because of sexual content, got sexually aroused by his lover's:

A. six toes on each foot
B. unwashed underwear
C. tattooed buttocks

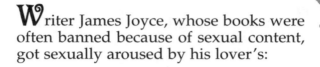

B. James Joyce got sexually aroused by his lover's unwashed underwear.

The term Peeping Tom was coined when a boy peeked at:

A. the naked Queen Elizabeth I

B. the naked Lady Godiva

C. the naked Lady Diana Spencer

❦❦❦❦❦❦❦

B. Peeping Tom was a boy who peeked at Lady Godiva as she rode naked on her horse through Coventry, covered only by her long hair.

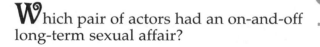

Which pair of actors had an on-and-off long-term sexual affair?

    A. Al Pacino and Dustin Hoffman
    B. Laurence Olivier and Danny Kaye
    C. Emilio Estevez and Charlie Sheen

⊚⊚⊚⊚⊚⊚⊚

B. Laurence Olivier and Danny Kaye had an on-and-off long-term sexual affair.

The number one advice to Victorian brides of that sexually repressive era was:

A. marry young and sin not

B. save yourself for your husband and from Hell

C. close your eyes and think of England

🌀🌀🌀🌀🌀🌀🌀

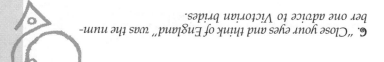

C. "Close your eyes and think of England" was the number one advice to Victorian brides.

The Oneida community in New York State:

    A. dissolved every marriage after two years

    B. allowed homosexual marriage

    C. gave each man marital privileges with every woman

🌀🌀🌀🌀🌀🌀🌀

C. In the 1800s, the Oneida community gave each man marital privileges with every woman.

Adolf Hitler ordered that, in a movie, any female character who broke up a marriage:

A. must die before the end
B. must be a Jew
C. must be a communist

🌀🌀🌀🌀🌀🌀🌀

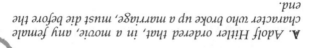

A. Adolf Hitler ordered that, in a movie, any female character who broke up a marriage, must die before the end.

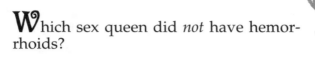

Which sex queen did *not* have hemorrhoids?

   A. Marilyn Monroe

   B. Elizabeth Taylor

   C. Mae West

@@@@@@@

C. Health-minded teetotaler Mae West did not have hemorrhoids while Marilyn Monroe and Elizabeth Taylor did.

Singer Bobby Darin said that Elvis Presley told him he considered marrying:

A. his favorite singer, Barbra Streisand

B. Mary Tyler Moore, who proposed to him

C. super-endowed Ann-Margret

@ @ @ @ @ @ @

C. Bobby Darin said that Elvis Presley once told him he considered marrying Ann-Margret.

Maypole dances were part of:

A. marriage ceremonies
B. fertility festivals
C. Satanic sexual rituals

🌀🌀🌀🌀🌀🌀🌀

B. *Maypole dances were part of fertility festivals, the maypole being a phallic symbol.*

Why did the two writers of erotica, Henry Miller and Anaïs Nin, go to a brothel together?

A. to watch a lesbian act
B. to get information for a story
C. to seek employment

๑๑๑๑๑๑๑

A. Henry Miller and Anaïs Nin went to a brothel to watch a lesbian act.

Rita Jenrette, before posing nude for *Playboy* magazine, said she and her congressman husband had made love:

A. in a White House bathroom
B. in the Statue of Liberty
C. on the steps of the Capitol Building

C. Rita Jenrette claimed she and her congressman husband had made love on the steps of the Capitol Building, wrapped in her fur coat and facing the Library of Congress.

Painter Vincent van Gogh lived sexually with just one woman, and she was:

A. a prostitute
B. a triple amputee
C. blind with just one ear

🌀 🌀 🌀 🌀 🌀 🌀 🌀

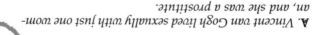

A. Vincent van Gogh lived sexually with just one woman, and she was a prostitute.

Which actress did *not* have a homosexual husband?

A. Judy Garland
B. Liza Minnelli
C. Doris Day

ⓖⓖⓖⓖⓖⓖⓖ

C. *Doris Day did not have a homosexual husband, but Judy Garland and her daughter Liza Minnelli did. Judy married director Vincent Minnelli; Liza wed performer Peter Allen.*

Actor Ted Danson, star of the TV comedy "Cheers," publicly made jokes about the private parts of his then-girlfriend:

A. Shelly Long
B. Bridget Fonda
C. Whoopi Goldberg

☻☻☻☻☻☻☻

C. Ted Danson publicly made jokes about the private parts of Whoopi Goldberg, which didn't bother her in the least.

Indian fighter Major Reno, who served under General George Custer, was court-martialed for:

A. having sexual relations with his horse

B. peeking through the window at the daughter of an officer

C. wearing women's underwear in battle

🌀 🌀 🌀 🌀 🌀 🌀 🌀

B. *Major Reno was court-martialed for peeking through the window at the daughter of an officer.*

Which country's pornography is mostly about sexual innocence infringed, like the sexual yielding of virginal schoolgirls and new brides?

    A. Australia
    B. Japan
    C. Russia

☺☺☺☺☺☺☺

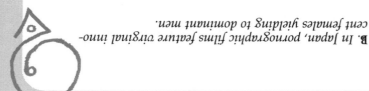

B. *In Japan, pornographic films feature virginal innocent females yielding to dominant men.*

Which of these terms is *not* another name for a prostitute?

   A. harlot
   B. strumpet
   C. shrew

◎◎◎◎◎◎◎

C. *Shrew is not another name for a prostitute, but harlot and strumpet are.*

Before getting married, rock star Billy Joel and super-model Christie Brinkley:

A. checked into hotels as Rocky and Sandy Shore

B. made love in a barrel half-filled with beer

C. made nude videos of each other

A. Before getting married, Billy Joel and Christie Brinkley used to check into hotels as Rocky and Sandy Shore.

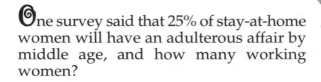

One survey said that 25% of stay-at-home women will have an adulterous affair by middle age, and how many working women?

A. 25%

B. 35%

C. 50%

@@@@@@@

C. *This same survey said that one-half of working women will have an adulterous affair by middle age.*

Baseball Hall of Famer, Reggie Jackson:

A. suffered from an illness that kept him in a perpetual state of sexual arousal

B. peeked under hotel doors with mirrors

C. said that he'd rather hit than have sex

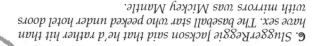

C. *Slugger Reggie Jackson said that he'd rather hit than have sex. The baseball star who peeked under hotel doors with mirrors was Mickey Mantle.*

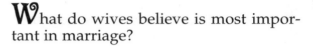

What do wives believe is most important in marriage?

    A. good sex

    B. hugging and kissing

    C. good cooking

♾♾♾♾♾♾

B. *According to Ladies' Home Journal, wives believe that hugging and kissing are most important in marriage.*

Actress Kathleen Turner says that when she's hot, if a man doesn't look at her:

A. he's gay
B. he's blind
C. she'll feel crushed

🌀🌀🌀🌀🌀🌀🌀

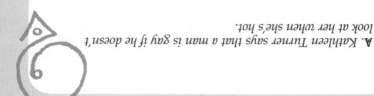

A. *Kathleen Turner says that a man is gay if he doesn't look at her when she's hot.*

Mormon leader Brigham Young died:

A. and his brother inherited his wife
B. along with his wife, while having sex
C. and left seventeen wives behind

⊚⊚⊚⊚⊚⊚⊚

C. When Mormon leader Brigham Young died, he had fathered fifty-six children, and left behind seventeen wives.

The ever-outrageous Roseanne:

A. said that both her husbands had been "too small" to satisfy her

B. had sex with her high school principal in order to become a cheerleader

C. had "Property of Tom Arnold" tattooed on her derriere

🌀🌀🌀🌀🌀🌀🌀

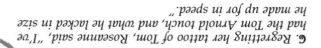

C. Regretting her tattoo of Tom, Roseanne said, "I've had the Tom Arnold touch, and what he lacked in size he made up for in speed."

The smallest recorded bust size of a Miss America is:

A. 32 inches
B. 30 inches
C. 28 inches

⊚⊚⊚⊚⊚⊚⊚

B. The smallest recorded bust size of a Miss America is thirty inches.

The largest recorded bust size of a Miss America is:

A. 37 inches
B. 39 inches
C. 41 inches

@ @ @ @ @ @ @

A. The largest recorded bust size of a Miss America is thirty-seven inches.

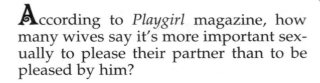

According to *Playgirl* magazine, how many wives say it's more important sexually to please their partner than to be pleased by him?

    A. 1 out of 4
    B. 2 out of 4
    C. 3 out of 4

@@@@@@@

C. *According to Playgirl, three out of four wives say it's more important to please their partner than to be pleased by him.*

W. Somerset Maugham, who wrote *Of Human Bondage*:

A. adopted his lover as his son

B. could only write when he was in love

C. got out of the army by dating an army psychiatrist

🌀🌀🌀🌀🌀🌀🌀

A. W. Somerset Maugham adopted his lover as his son in order to disown his daughter Elizabeth.

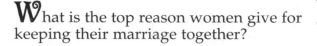

What is the top reason women give for keeping their marriage together?

    A. "We agree about our sex life."
    B. "Marriage is sacred."
    C. "My spouse is my best friend."

@@@@@@@

C. *According to Psychology Today, "My spouse is my best friend" is the top reason women give for keeping their marriage together.*

The time during a woman's menstrual cycle when she's *least* likely to become pregnant is called:

A. the hallelujah time

B. the barren period

C. the safe period

🌀🌀🌀🌀🌀🌀

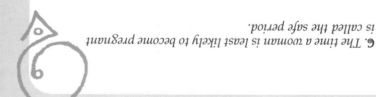

C. *The time a woman is least likely to become pregnant is called the safe period.*

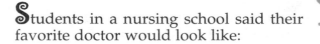

Students in a nursing school said their favorite doctor would look like:

A. Regis Philbin
B. Jonas Salk
C. Mel Gibson

⊚ ⊚ ⊚ ⊚ ⊚ ⊚ ⊚

C. Nursing school students said their favorite doctor would look like Mel Gibson, be as intelligent as Jonas Salk, and as professionally pleasant as Regis Philbin.

$\mathbb{Y}$ou can get the most money for a letter written by which sex icon?

A. Elvis Presley
B. Marilyn Monroe
C. Rudolph Valentino

@@@@@@@

B. You can get the most money for a letter written by sex icon Marilyn Monroe, a notorious nonwriter.

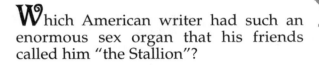

Which American writer had such an enormous sex organ that his friends called him "the Stallion"?

A. Ernest Hemingway
B. Jack London
C. John Steinbeck

ⓒⓒⓒⓒⓒⓒⓒ

B. *Novelist Jack London, who wrote* Call of the Wild, *was called "the Stallion" by his friends, who were in awe of his equine sex organ.*

Philandering film star Charlie Chaplin had to pay child support even though:

A. Charlie had had a vasectomy
B. the blood test proved Charlie wasn't the father
C. Charlie said he didn't do it and would never do it again

⊚⊚⊚⊚⊚⊚⊚

B. *Charlie Chaplin had to pay child support even though the blood test proved he wasn't the father because the jury wanted to punish him for his habit of deflowering young girls.*

According to Hollywood writer James Bacon, who did the Mafia keep from marrying sex star Kim Novak?

A. Sammy Davis, Jr.
B. Joe Di Maggio
C. Elvis Presley

ⓖⓖⓖⓖⓖⓖⓖ

A. According to James Bacon, the Mafia kept Sammy Davis, Jr., from marrying Kim Novak.

$\mathbf{T}$he term *carnal knowledge* means:

   A. pornography
   B. sexual intercourse
   C. any sexual deviation

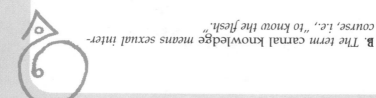

B. *The term* carnal knowledge *means sexual intercourse, i.e., "to know the flesh."*

A *bull dyke* is:

A. a very masculine lesbian
B. a man with a very large sex organ
C. a transvestite

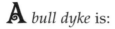

A. A **bull dyke** *is a very masculine lesbian, ultra-mannish in appearance and attitude.*

Who was the top pinup sex queen of the 1940s?

    A. Jean Harlow
    B. Marilyn Monroe
    C. Betty Grable

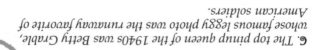

C. *The top pinup queen of the 1940s was Betty Grable, whose famous leggy photo was the runaway favorite of American soldiers.*

In Massachusetts in the 1600s, a teenage boy confessed to having sex with two horses, two cows, and four sheep. He was then:

A. banished to the wilderness

B. made to sleep in the barn

C. executed

⊚⊚⊚⊚⊚⊚⊚

C. *Several hundred years ago in Massachusetts, a teenage boy was executed for having sex with two horses, two cows, and four sheep.*

Lawrence of Arabia, when not leading battles in the desert, preferred in sex:

A. to deflower virgins

B. to be beaten by men

C. to observe copulating camels

@@@@@@@

B. *Lawrence of Arabia preferred to be severely beaten by men during sexual activities.*

Bangkok, the Asian center of sex tourism, got its biggest boost from:

A. Japanese businessmen

B. American GIs from the Vietnam War

C. homosexuals worldwide

🌀🌀🌀🌀🌀🌀🌀

B. *Bangkok got its biggest boost from American GIs from the Vietnam War.*

Who said that his best customers for black Harlem prostitutes were white officials: politicians, preachers, and police-men?

A. Malcolm X
B. Don Corleone
C. John Gotti

๑๑๑๑๑๑๑

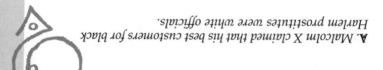

A. Malcolm X claimed that his best customers for black Harlem prostitutes were white officials.

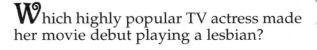

Which highly popular TV actress made her movie debut playing a lesbian?

- **A.** Candice Bergen
- **B.** Roseanne
- **C.** Mary Tyler Moore

☺☺☺☺☺☺☺

A. *Candice Bergen of "Murphy Brown" made her movie debut playing a lesbian in The Group.*

The professional most likely to have sexual contact with a client is:

A. a psychotherapist

B. a lawyer

C. a dentist

☉☉☉☉☉☉☉

A. A psychotherapist is most likely to have sexual contact with a client.

When are women's dreams more likely to contain sexual anxiety and hostility?

    A. right after sex
    B. when sex has been absent
    C. right before menstruation

C. Women's dreams are more likely to contain sexual anxiety and hostility right before menstruation.

At the White House, United States President Warren G. Harding made love to his mistress:

- **A**. in the Rose Garden
- **B**. in a closet
- **C**. in the kitchen

⑨⑨⑨⑥⑨⑥⑨

B. *President Harding made love to his mistress in a closet, a fact that President Kennedy often chuckled over.*

Homosexual men who pursue young boys are called:

A. eagle scouts
B. chicken hawks
C. tufted titmice

B. Homosexual men who pursue young boys are called chicken hawks.

The word *eunuch,* which describes a castrated man, originally meant:

A. abandoned by God
B. the guardian of the bed
C. where did it go?

〰〰〰〰〰〰〰

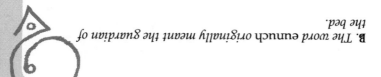
B. *The word eunuch originally meant the guardian of the bed.*

In Argentina, Eva Perón hated the nickname the public gave her. She was called:

A. The Little Whore
B. The Sexy Social Climber
C. The Bitch Goddess of the Bedroom

W**hen Alan Clark, former British defense minister, was caught in an affair with a judge's wife and her two daughters, he said:**

A. "I can't help it, I'm addicted to sex."
B. "The Devil made me do it."
C. "I should be horsewhipped."

⑨⑨⑨⑨⑨⑨⑨

C. When Alan Clark was caught in an affair with a judge's wife and her two daughters, he said, "I should be horsewhipped."

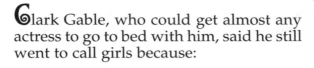

Clark Gable, who could get almost any actress to go to bed with him, said he still went to call girls because:

A. "I can pay them to go away."
B. "I've done all the actresses."
C. "They know how to do it."

⊚⊚⊚⊚⊚⊚⊚

A. Clark Gable said he continued to visit call girls because "I can pay them to go away."

In Rome, if the vestal virgins broke their vows of virginity, they were punished by death. These vows lasted:

A. six years
B. thirty years
C. a lifetime

⊚⊚⊚⊚⊚⊚⊚

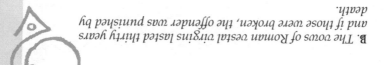

B. *The vows of Roman vestal virgins lasted thirty years and if those were broken, the offender was punished by death.*

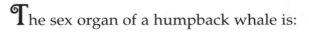

The sex organ of a humpback whale is:

    A. the same length as a man's
    B. ten times as long as a man's
    C. twenty times as long as a man's

⊙ ⊙ ⊙ ⊙ ⊙ ⊙ ⊙

C. *The sex organ of a humpback whale is twenty times as long as that of a man.*

The sex organ of a gorilla is:

    A. one-third the length of a man's
    B. the same length as a man's
    C. three times as long as a man's

A. The sex organ of a man is three times as long as a gorilla's.

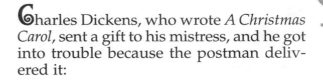

Charles Dickens, who wrote *A Christmas Carol*, sent a gift to his mistress, and he got into trouble because the postman delivered it:

- **A.** to his other mistress
- **B.** to Mrs. Dickens
- **C.** to his best friend's wife

⊚⊚⊚⊚⊚⊚⊚

B. Charles Dickens sent a gift to his mistress, but the postman delivered it to his wife by mistake.

How many prostitutes have been victims of incest?

A. about 1 out of 4
B. about 1 out of 3
C. about 1 out of 2

❊❊❊❊❊❊❊

C. *About one out of two prostitutes has been a victim of incest.*

Which media "bad girl" was pictured in *Penthouse* magazine, completely nude, in various active sexual positions?

A. Amy Fisher
B. Tonya Harding
C. Lorena Bobbitt

☺☺☺☺☺☺☺

B. "Bad girl" Tonya Harding was pictured completely nude in Penthouse magazine.

Censors told Hitchcock to cut part of the famous shower scene in *Psycho* because of nudity. He returned the shower scene to the censors and it passed:

- **A.** because the scene had been filmed again
- **B.** because one-tenth of a second had been cut
- **C.** even though Hitchcock had not changed it

🌀🌀🌀🌀🌀🌀🌀

C. *Hitchcock returned the shower scene to the censors and it passed, even though Hitchcock had not changed it.*

Tennis champion Big Bill Tilden, who never undressed in the locker room, had a sex life that:

- **A.** basically consisted of fondling boys
- **B.** basically existed under the influence of opium
- **C.** was basically limited to men with whips

✆✆✆✆✆✆

A. *Big Bill Tilden's sex life basically consisted of fondling boys. He spent seven months in prison for fondling a fourteen-year-old boy.*

When the jealous actor W. C. Fields paid a private eye to follow his girlfriend:

A. she hid out in a brothel

B. she was caught with her lesbian lover

C. she married the private eye

☙❦☙❦☙❦☙

C. When W. C. Fields paid a private eye to follow his girlfriend, she married the private eye.

What does a famous tabloid photograph show Fergie, the Duchess of York, and her American financial advisor doing?

    A. studying bank balances in the nude
    B. him sucking her toes
    C. each wearing the other's clothes

B. *A famous tabloid photograph shows Sarah Ferguson having her toes sucked by her American financial advisor.*

$\mathbf{I}$n the world of prostitution, which is the bottom-ranked job?

- **A.** call girl
- **B.** brothel girl
- **C.** bar girl

@@@@@@@@

C. In the world of prostitution, bar girl is the bottom-ranked job.

In Latin, the word *negligee* means:

   A. I show what I have
   B. I'm always ready
   C. don't clean the house

@ @ @ @ @ @ @

How did sex star Kim Basinger, of the movie *Batman*, lighten up after losing an eight-million-dollar law suit and going bankrupt?

A. she hired a boy-toy for a two-week sexual fling

B. she married Alec Baldwin

C. she got her breasts enlarged

☙☙☙☙☙☙☙

B. *After losing an eight-million-dollar law suit, Kim Basinger lightened up by marrying Alec Baldwin.*

Among romance writers, who is called the Queen of Love?

A. Fabio
B. Danielle Steel
C. Barbara Cartland

@@@@@@@

C. *In the romance writing community, Barbara Cartland is called the Queen of Love. She is related to the ruling family of Britain, and she has authored hundreds of romances.*

When French actress Sarah Bernhardt was not having one of her thousand sexual affairs, she often:

A. slept with her forty-one cats

B. slept in the bathtub

C. slept in a coffin

๑๑๑๑๑๑๑

C. *Sarah Bernhardt often slept in her coffin when she was not having one of her many affairs. She said, "I have been one of the great lovers of my century."*

Actor Charles Laughton, star of *The Hunchback of Notre Dame*, preferred that his male lovers be:

    A. young and in need of money
    B. old and rich
    C. crippled and ugly

                           ᕯ ᕯ ᕯ ᕯ ᕯ ᕯ ᕯ

A. *Charles Laughton preferred that his male lovers be young and in need of money. He usually had to pay because, as he said, "I have got a face like an elephant's behind."*

The Mayflower Madam said that among her high-priced call girls, the redheads were:

A. desired more than blondes
B. desired about the same as blondes
C. not desired at all

C. The Mayflower Madam said that among her high-priced call girls, the redheads were not desired at all.

Rob Camilletti lived with his lover, who was twenty-three years older, named:

A. Marilyn Monroe
B. Cher
C. Rock Hudson

@@@@@@@

B. Rob Camilletti's lover was Cher. Cher's first husband, Sonny Bono, is now a U.S. congressman.

Writer Ernest Hemingway bragged that he had sex with which spy?

A. Tokyo Rose

B. Mata Hari

C. Natasha Boris

⊚ ⊚ ⊚ ⊚ ⊚ ⊚ ⊚

B. Ernest Hemingway bragged that he had sex with the spy Mata Hari. Ernest was quite a braggart when it came to sex, but this might be true because she began her career as a prostitute.

The term *cruise* means:

   A. to have sex in a moving automobile
   B. to oil your body before sex
   C. to actively look for a sex partner

ⓒ ⓒ ⓒ ⓒ ⓒ ⓒ ⓒ

C. *The term cruise means to actively look for a sex partner.*

The aphrodisiac made from cantharides is known as:

A. Portuguese dragon
B. French flower
C. Spanish fly

@@@@@@@

C. The aphrodisiac made from cantharides is Spanish fly, and it was a favorite of the infamous Marquis de Sade.

Before writing *Tom Sawyer* and *Huckleberry Finn*, Mark Twain fell in love with his wife when he first saw her:

A. in a photograph
B. in a striptease show
C. through a crack in the bathroom door

A. Mark Twain fell in love with his wife when he first saw her in a photograph and decided to marry her.

Before Marla Maples married Donald Trump, what was stolen from her to be used for sexual purposes?

A. her falsies

B. her shoes

C. her soiled underwear

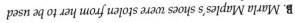

B. *Marla Maples's shoes were stolen from her to be used for sexual purposes.*

Sexy actress Raquel Welch said:

A. I am not and never will be a sex object

B. I love being a world famous sex object

C. I'm the only actress who turned Elvis down

〰〰〰〰〰〰〰

B. Raquel Welch said, "I love being a world famous sex object." She also said, "All those stories that have been written and rumored about my having had silicone injections to bring out my bust are totally false."

Unicorns, mythical white horses with a single horn, could only be caught:

A. by female virgins

B. by giving them a love potion

C. by sprinkling salt on their sex organs

A. *Only female virgins could catch the mythical white unicorns.*

What did American-born Josephine Baker wear in the Folies Bergère when she scandalized Paris?

A. just a bra made of coconut shells

B. just a belt ringed with bananas

C. just a pair of ruby red slippers

🌀🌀🌀🌀🌀🌀🌀

B. *Josephine Baker scandalized Paris by wearing just a belt ringed with bananas. She was the first African-American woman to gain international celebrity.*

Before he became President of the United States, who was impotent in his first two attempts at adultery?

A. Dwight D. Eisenhower
B. John F. Kennedy
C. Lyndon B. Johnson

⊚⊚⊚⊚⊚⊚⊚

A. Dwight D. Eisenhower was impotent in his first two attempts at adultery.

Saint Agnes, whose day is January 20, is the patron saint of:

A. all married couples

B. prostitutes

C. young virgins

C. *Saint Agnes is the patron saint of young virgins.*

When the groom is forced to marry, usually by the father of a pregnant girl, it is called:

    A. a ball-and-chain marriage
    B. a dance with the Devil
    C. a shotgun wedding

@ @ @ @ @ @ @

C. As Eddie Albert said in the movie Oklahoma, "I wanted to marry her when I saw the moonlight shining on the barrel of her father's shotgun."

Dr. Sigmund Freud's *Electra complex* refers to:

   A. a wife's desire to breastfeed her husband

   B. a diminishment of sexual charisma due to latent homosexuality

   C. the sexual attraction a little girl feels toward her father

ⓖⓖⓖⓖⓖⓖⓖ

C. *Freud's Electra complex refers to the sexual attraction a little girl feels toward her father.*

In Tuscany, the missionary position of face-to-face, man-on-top is called:

A. the king and queen position
B. the Devil's position
C. the angelic position

⊚⊚⊚⊚⊚⊚⊚

C. What Americans call the missionary position is called the angelic position in Tuscany (central Italy).

The nickname of French sex goddess Brigitte Bardot is:

A. The Wild Cat

B. The Sex Kitten

C. Le Pussy Cat

@@@@@@@

B. Brigitte Bardot's nickname was The Sex Kitten because she often played a man-teaser who found it hard to resist temptation. She was directed in her sexiest movies by husband Roger Vadim, who later married Jane Fonda.

Which sexy couple did *not* marry each other twice?

   A. Richard Burton and Elizabeth Taylor
   B. Don Johnson and Melanie Griffith
   C. Elvis and Priscilla Presley

@@@@@@@

C. *Elvis and Priscilla Presley did not marry each other again, while Richard Burton and Elizabeth Taylor did, as did Don Johnson and Melanie Griffith.*

At age thirteen, who sat in a car with her first date, while he nonchalantly passed gas?

A. the dignified Jackie Kennedy
B. lavender-eyed Elizabeth Taylor
C. America's *Pretty Woman* Julia Roberts

ⓖⓖⓖⓖⓖⓖⓖ

C. *On her first date, Julia Roberts sat in a car while her escort nonchalantly passed gas.*

How often do men become sexually aroused while dreaming?

A. rarely
B. in about half their dreams
C. nearly every time they dream

🌀🌀🌀🌀🌀🌀🌀

C. Men become sexually aroused nearly every time they dream.

$\mathbf{W}$e hear the line, "Why can't a woman be more like a man?" in a musical called:

   A. *My Fair Lady*
   B. *Camelot*
   C. *Kiss Me Kate*

☙☙☙☙☙☙☙

A. *In* My Fair Lady *we hear the line, "Why can't a woman be more like a man?"*

Singer Alice Cooper and actress Linda Blair went on a date:

- **A.** to a brothel
- **B.** to a nudist camp
- **C.** to see the movie *The Exorcist*

๑๑๑๑๑๑๑

C. Alice and Linda went on a date to see the movie in which she was starring, wherein she performs a sexual act on herself with a crucifix.

A *People* magazine poll says, in its first twenty years, the sexiest man is:

A. Luke Perry
B. Mel Gibson
C. Bill Clinton

꩜ ꩜ ꩜ ꩜ ꩜ ꩜ ꩜

B. A People magazine poll rated Mel Gibson as the sexiest man. Mel had his hind end shaved so he could show it off in Lethal Weapon 2.

According to a *Seventeen* magazine poll, how many teen girls expect future husbands to share household duties?

A. 3 out of 10

B. 6 out of 10

C. 9 out of 10

☺☺☺☺☺☺☺

6. *Nine out of ten teen girls expect future husbands to share household duties.*

In the ancient Greek play *Lysistrata*, the wives try to get the husbands to stop going to war by:

A. threatening to become lesbians

B. threatening to mutilate the men's sex organs

C. withholding sex

C. In *Lysistrata*, the wives withhold sex to get their husbands to stop the war.

According to *Cosmopolitan* magazine, which vibrator is most frequently recommended by sex therapists?

A. the Hitachi Magic Wand
B. the New York Yankee Power Hitter
C. the Smith & Wesson Overnighter

@@@@@@@

A. According to Cosmopolitan, the Hitachi Magic Wand is the vibrator most frequently recommended by sex therapists.

After Charles Manson murdered his wife, director Roman Polanski fled the United States after pleading guilty to:

- A. raping one of the Charles Manson gang
- B. fondling boys while he was a substitute Sunday school teacher
- C. unlawful sexual intercourse with a thirteen-year-old girl

@@@@@@@

C. *Roman Polanski pleaded guilty to unlawful sexual intercourse with a girl of thirteen. Later he said, "For some reason, young girls like me."*

Which sexy singer did Travis Tritt say reduced country music to a butt-wiggling contest?

A. Reba McEntire
B. Garth Brooks
C. Billy Ray Cyrus

@@@@@@@

6. *Country singer Travis Tritt said that Billy Ray Cyrus reduced country music to a butt-wiggling contest.*

Billionaire Howard Hughes invented this term to describe sex star Jean Harlow:

A. platinum blond
B. sex bombshell
C. sex goddess

🌀🌀🌀🌀🌀🌀🌀

A. Howard Hughes called Jean Harlow platinum blond to publicize the movie Hell's Angels, in which Harlow brought the house down with her sexy delivery of: "Pardon me while I slip into something more comfortable."

Who claimed to have made love in a canoe, on a fire escape, and in a telephone booth?

A. Clark Gable
B. Elvis Presley
C. John F. Kennedy

@@@@@@@

A. Clark Gable claimed to have made love in a canoe, on a fire escape, and in a telephone booth. But his wife Carole Lombard said, "To tell the honest truth, he isn't such a helluva good lay."

Mozart knew so little about sexual affairs, that for help on an opera he called in an expert, the famous lover:

A. Casanova
B. Salieri
C. Don Juan

🌀🌀🌀🌀🌀🌀🌀

A. Mozart knew so little about sexual affairs that he called in the famous lover Casanova for his sexual expertise.

Prostitutes were nicknamed after a Union officer named:

    A. General Joseph Hooker

    B. Major Anthony Harlot

    C. General Jeb Strumpet

⊙ ⊙ ⊙ ⊙ ⊙ ⊙ ⊙

A. In 1864, prostitutes were nicknamed after a Union officer named General Joseph Hooker. They followed his troops and were called Hooker's Girls.

Basketball Hall of Famer Wilt Chamberlain put himself in the Sexual Hall of Fame by claiming to have slept with:

A. 4,000 women
B. 11,000 women
C. 20,000 women

☙☙☙☙☙☙☙

C. Wilt Chamberlain claims to have slept with twenty thousand women.

What glandular secretion of worker bees is much in demand because it is thought to help increase human male sex drive?

A. beeswax
B. bee pollen
C. royal jelly

@@@@@@@@

C. Royal jelly is thought to help increase the human male sex drive.

When Francisco de Goya's lover was unfaithful, he painted her:

A. with a man's sex organ
B. making love with a devil
C. with two faces

C. Francisco de Goya painted his lover with two faces after she cheated on him.

What do actresses Madonna, Ann-Margret, and Sally Field have in common?

- **A.** each was a former cheerleader
- **B.** each went to bed with her gym teacher
- **C.** each went to bed with Michael Jackson

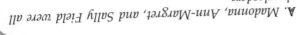

A. Madonna, Ann-Margret, and Sally Field were all cheerleaders.

Singer Anita Bryant said she was chosen by God to become "His vessel" in His war against:

A. rapists
B. marital infidelity
C. homosexuals

⊙⊙⊙⊙⊙⊙⊙

C. Anita Bryant said she was chosen by God to war against homosexuals. She said that if God favored homosexuality, the occupants of the Garden of Eden would have been named Adam and Bruce.

The founder of *Hustler*, a top-selling pornographic magazine, claimed to be:

A. a communist

B. a born-again Christian

C. a former prostitute

⊚⊚⊚⊚⊚⊚⊚

B. *Larry Flynt, the founder of* Hustler *claimed to be a born-again Christian, brought into the heavenly fold with the help of President Carter's sister.*

Before he was executed for treason, Sir Thomas More said that the bride and groom should do what before the wedding?

A. wear each other's clothes

B. fast and pray for sexual guidance

C. see each other naked

🌀🌀🌀🌀🌀🌀🌀

C. Sir Thomas More said that the bride and groom should see each other naked before the wedding.

Dian Parkinson, ex-model of "The Price Is Right," did *not:*

A. pose nude for *Playboy* magazine

B. charge game show host Bob Barker with making her perform sex

C. go to bed with Mick Jagger and David Bowie at the same time

@@@@@@@

C. *Dian Parkinson did not go to bed with Mick Jagger and David Bowie, but she did pose nude for Playboy and she did charge Bob Barker with making her perform sex.*

Mozart knew so little about sexual affairs, that for help on an opera he called in an expert, the famous lover:

    A. Casanova
    B. Salieri
    C. Don Juan

@@@@@@@

A. Mozart knew so little about sexual affairs that he called in the famous lover Casanova for his sexual expertise.

The names of these towns have sexual connotations: Beaver, Blue Ball, Hooker, Intercourse, and Little Gap, and they are all located in:

A. Alaska

B. Arkansas

C. Pennsylvania

C. Pennsylvania contains the towns of Beaver, Blue Ball, Hooker, Intercourse, and Little Gap.

Attila the Hun died:

- **A.** while making love
- **B.** from an arrow shot through his genitals
- **C.** from a sexual disease

A. Attila the Hun died while making love, and thus Europe was spared destruction.

Wolfgang Amadeus Mozart, at age twenty-five:

A. was still a virgin

B. upon threat of death, was buggered by Francis II

C. used a gold-and-ivory dildo as a metronome

⊚⊚⊚⊚⊚⊚⊚

A. At age twenty-five, Mozart was still a virgin because, as he wrote to his father, he had "too much dread and fear of diseases."

The most commercially successful pornographic movie of all time is:

  A. *Deep Throat*
  B. *You, Devil, You*
  C. *Debbie Does Dallas*

A. *The porno movie Deep Throat cost less than fifty thousand dollars to make, and it has brought in more than 100 million dollars.*

French painter Toulouse-Lautrec preferred living:

A. with large-breasted African women
B. with sexually precocious young boys
C. in a brothel

🌀🌀🌀🌀🌀🌀🌀

C. Toulouse-Lautrec preferred living in a brothel, where
he was thought to be in the running for man-with-the-
largest-sex-organ-in-Paris.

National Condom Day:

A. is celebrated on Valentine's Day in America

B. is celebrated on May Day in Russia and the Ukraine

C. was vigorously vetoed by President Ronald Reagan

〰〰〰〰〰〰〰

A. In the United States, National Condom Day is celebrated on Valentine's Day.

Knute Rockne, Notre Dame football coach, got the idea for his famous football formation (the Four Horsemen's Back Shift) while:

A. watching four Chicago prostitutes sexually service his backfield

B. watching a chorus line in a girlie show

C. watching prostitutes perform as pantyless cheerleaders

〰〰〰〰〰〰〰

B. *While watching a chorus line in a girlie show, Knute Rockne got the idea for the Four Horsemen's Back Shift.*

Actor Charlie Sheen spent $50,000-plus:

A. on Hollywood madam Heidi Fleiss's high-priced prostitutes

B. to cure the sexual diseases he got from various prostitutes

C. to pay his future wife's fines for her activities as a Sunset Strip prostitute

🌀🌀🌀🌀🌀🌀🌀🌀

A. For the services of Heidi Fleiss's prostitutes, Charlie Sheen spent more than $50,000.

Gennifer Flowers, in her book *Passion and Betrayal*, claims that:

A. Bill Clinton loved to dress up like Hillary, pretending he was in charge
B. she used to tie Bill Clinton to the bedpost to maximize his sexual excitability
C. Bill Clinton got his jollies by licking champagne off her body

☙☙☙☙☙☙☙

B. *Gennifer Flowers claims that she used to tie the Bill Clinton to the bedpost to maximize his sexual excitement! She also claims to be much superior to Hillary when it comes to sex.*

Barbra Streisand has had sex with:

A. Mick Jagger
B. John Lennon
C. Elvis Presley

C. *In his book Streisand:* Her Life, *James Spada claims that according to a Presley spokesperson, Babs and the king had a one-night stand in Las Vegas in 1969.*

To support her brother Michael, Janet Jackson wore a shirt at the MTV awards that said:

A. "Pervert 2"
B. "2 Love Children Is Godly"
C. "2 For Love"

@@@@@@@

A. Janet Jackson wore a shirt at the MTV awards that said, "Pervert 2," presumably to support her brother Michael and to poke fun at the media.